Piano Solo

W I N D H A M   H

Piano Sampler

Cover Photo by Steve Solinsky

ISBN 978-0-7935-2358-0

HAL•LEONARD®
CORPORATION
7777 W. BLUEMOUND RD. P.O. BOX 13819 MILWAUKEE, WI 53213

WINDHAM HILL RECORDS

Windham Hill is an independent record label, in partnership with the Bertelsmann Music Group (BMG). Based in Northern California, Windham Hill has developed a diverse catalog of instrumental recordings. This first piano folio, along with its sister folio for guitar, features mostly earlier works from a variety of the label's artists.

While many styles of contemporary piano are transcribed within these pages, there is a common thread that weaves through each selection: the enduring power and beauty of a song, a melody, and a theme that evokes imagery and emotion.

Windham Hill recordings are available at your local retail store or through:
Sound Delivery: 800-888-8574
Tower Records: 800-648-4844

The Windham Hill Records Information Line (illustrated below) is your link to information on your favorite artists, including concert itineraries, new releases, and sheet music. If you aren't already on the Windham Hill mailing list, you can leave your name and address by calling the Information Line, or send a postcard to:

Windham Hill Records
Consumer Relations Dept.
Post Office Box 9388
Stanford, CA 94309

The Windham Hill Records Information Line
800-888-8544

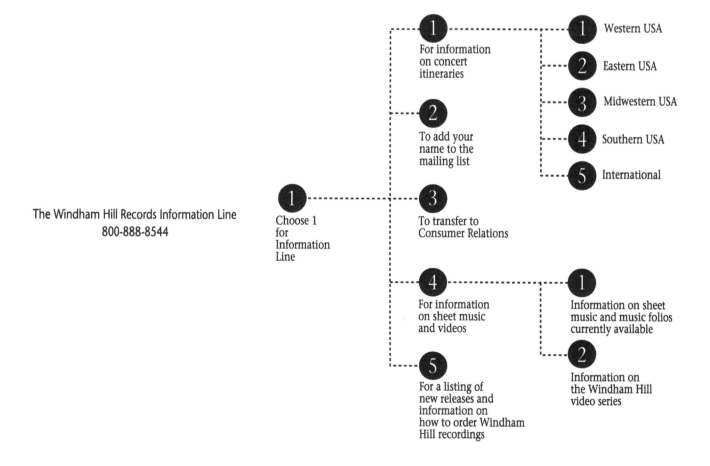

Photo by John F. Cooper

PHILIP AABERG

A Leonard Bernstein music scholarship took Phil to Harvard, where his classical training led him to Pulitzer Prize-winning composer, Leo Kirchner's chamber music seminar, earning him an invitation to play at the Marlboro Chamber Festival under the scrutiny of Pablo Casals and Rudolf Serkin. His hard edged, superb pianistic techniques always support the deeply felt emotion of his music. Phil has toured and recorded with such name artists as Peter Gabriel, John Hiatt, and Elvin Bishop.

Discography

High Plains - 1037
The Shape Of The Land (soundtrack) - 1055
Out Of The Frame - 1069
Upright - 1088
Cinema - 11110

Discography

Wind Dance - 1016
Islands - 1033
Reunion - 1049
Still Moments - 0086
She Describes Infinity - 1063
Switchback - 1081
A Windham Hill Retrospective - 11112
Stained Glass Memories - 11120

SCOTT COSSU

Scott has consistently recorded a distinctive melodic blend of jazz, classical and ethnic influences with a panorama of deep emotions. Scott has studied classical piano, music theory and composition, as well as ethnic music ranging from the Andes to the Far East. His musical collaborations are many, including guitarist Van Manakas, flutist Dave Valentin, bassist Mark Egan and cellists Eugene Friesen and David Darling.

Photo by Steve Bloom

Photo by Kent Phillips

MALCOLM DALGL·ISH

Malcolm is a virtuoso hammer dulcimer player and composer who has merged his

background in choir, theater, and folk music to bring new and exciting performances to

families and communities. Formerly with the group Metamora, Malcolm is a widely

acclaimed artist and performer.

Photo by Kent Phillips

Discography

Jogging The Memory - 1046
Morning Walk (Metamora) - 1068

Discography

Something Of Time (Nightnoise) - 1057
At The End Of The Evening (Nightnoise) - 1076
The Parting Tide (Nightnoise) - 1097
A Windham Hill Retrospective (Nightnoise) - 11111
Shadow Of Time (Nightnoise) - 11130

TRÍONA NÍ DHOMHNAILL

Formerly part of the renowned Bothy Band, Tríona now works with her brother,

Mícheal, and fellow artists Johnny Cunningham and Brian Dunning, in the Celtic

quartet, Nightnoise. Tríona brings a virtuosity on piano, synthesizer, accordion, whistle

and most recently, vocals, adding instrumental variety and flexibility to the band.

Photo by Kevin Laubaucher

BARBARA HIGBIE

Although Barbara has emerged in recent years as a singer-songwriter, she is best known

as the keyboardist in the acclaimed, and Grammy nominated ensemble, Montreux.

Barbara studied classical piano and composition, but her musical identity has evolved

from her deep interest in world music.

Photo by Steve Hathaway

Discography

Signs Of Life - 1090
Tideline (w/Darol Anger) - 1021
Live At Montreux (Montreux) - 1036
Sign Language (Montreux) - 1058
Let Them Say (Montreux) - 1084
A Windham Hill Retrospective - 11122
  (Montreux)

Discography

Unusual Weather - 1044
Toward The Center of the Night - 1083
Drastic Measures - 1102
Sign Language (Montreux) - 1058
Let them Say (Montreux) - 1084
A Windham Hill Retrospective - 11122
(Montreux)
Thonk - 10322

MICHAEL MANRING

Although primarily known for his remarkable innovative work as a bass guitarist, Michael

has also written piano compositions. He has long contributed as a session player,

collaborating with his fellow Windham Hill artists. Michael has also been an active

composer, both as a solo artist and as a member of the group, Montreux.

Photo by Rick English

BILL QUIST

Classically trained, Bill was one of the first artists to be signed to Windham Hill. His "Piano Solos Of Erik Satie" recording contributed to the label's growing keyboard repertoire. Bill studied with Jon Peterson at the Interlochen Arts Academy in Michigan, also in Paris and San Francisco. His music has been influenced by major composers, particularly of the romantic and impressionist eras.

Discography

Piano Solos Of Erik Satie - 1008

Discography

Usually/Always - 1071

FRED SIMON

The co-founder of the Simon and Bard group, which recorded three albums of mostly Simon originals, Fred has made four records of his music, and continues to compose for his own group, as well as for film, dance and TV. Fred has also recorded and/or performed with Ralph Towner, Paul McCandless, Larry Coryell, Lyle Mays, Ian Matthews, Jerry Goodman, Fareed Haque, Steve Rodby, Paul Wertico, Ross Traut, Bonnie Herman, Stan Kenton and others.

Photo by A. John Helyar

IRA STEIN

Inspired by Bach and Debussy, Ira studied classical piano, before being influenced by the

jazz improvisations of Keith Jarett and the group, Oregon. Ira attended an Oregon

workshop at the Naropa Institute, where he studied with his mentor, Ralph Towner.

While there, he met Russel Walder, and they formed the piano/oboe duo which signed

to Windham Hill.

Discography

Elements (w/Russel Walder) - 1020
Transit (w/Russel Walder) - 1042

Discography

Solid Colors - 1023
Unaccountable Effect - 1034
Escape Of The Circus Ponies - 1099
My Foolish Heart - 11115

LIZ STORY

Liz has established herself as one of the most distinctive composers and pianists of the

new instrumental music that emerged in the 1980's, and is often referred to as "The

Premier Female Artist of Contemporary Instrumental Music". She has recently recorded

"My Foolish Heart", an album of jazz standards with bassist Joel DiBartolo.

Photo by Steve Hathaway

Photo by Mark Packo

TIM STORY

This Ohio-based composer, arranger, musician and engineer views his keyboard style as modern chamber music, citing such diverse influences as Bela Bartok, Claude Debussy, Steve Reich and Miles Davis. Tim has garnered international attention for his music which ranges from solo acoustic piano to more orchestral works using electronic instruments.

Discography

Glass Green - 11124

THE GIFT

By PHILIP AABERG

DEVOTION

By LIZ STORY

Moderately, freely

* 12/8 and 9/8 in this piece remain in *duple* meter
(the beat is subdivided by two).

ENGRAVINGS

By IRA STEIN

Più mosso

HIGH PLAINS

By PHILIP AABERG

Simply

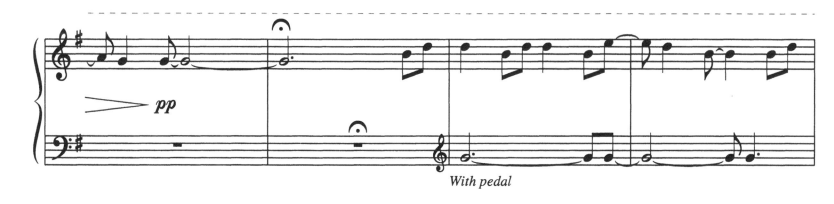

With pedal

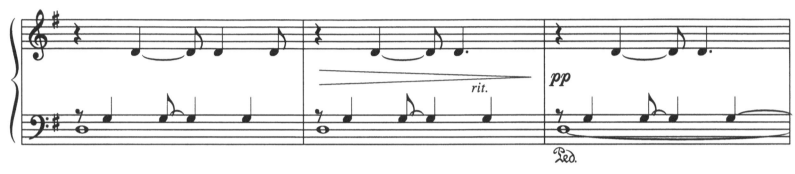

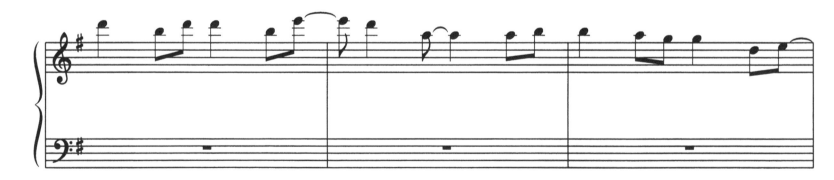

HUGH

By TRÍONA NÍ DHOMHNAILL

IN THIS SMALL SPOT

By TIM STORY

*Originally in the Key of G flat

LOU ANN

By PHILIP AABERG

* This piece is based on the characteristic decay and
resonance of the piano. Thus, the tempo will be dictated
by each particular instrument. This is a very interior
piece. Listen.

sempre p

* *Play fast, chromatic glissando down.*

LIFE IN THE TREES

By MICHAEL MANRING

Soulfully

43

mf
improvisation

Repeat and Fade

MANHATTAN UNDERGROUND

By SCOTT COSSU

*Originally in the Key of G# minor

50

Gm11

improvisation

mf

8vb through solo section

TRUE STORY

By BARBARA HIGBIE

56

NEW WALTZ

By MALCOLM DALGLISH

D.C. al Coda

CODA

Ped.

ORISTANO SOJOURN

By SCOTT COSSU

To Coda ⊕

PURPLE MOUNTAIN

By SCOTT COSSU

Tenderly

p

With pedal

* *Originally in the Key of D flat*

To Coda

SOLID COLORS

By LIZ STORY

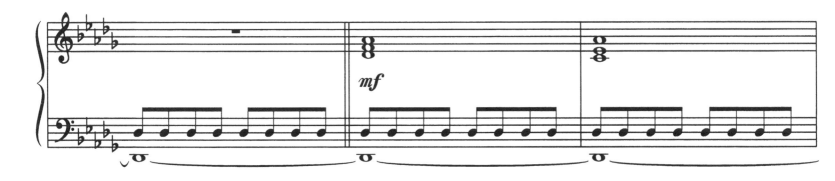

grad. dim.

pp

Rubato; a little more freely

mp

3

D.S. al Coda

CODA

GYMNOPÉDIE No. 1

(From "3 GYMNOPÉDIES")

By ERIK SATIE
Arranged by BILL QUIST

Slowly*

With pedal

* Original edition indicates "Lent et doulereux" which translates to "Slow and painful."

Try bringing out the E in the right hand (as melody), thus serving as a resolution of the F in the previous measure.

TIDELINE

By BARBARA HIGBIE

94

USUALLY/ALWAYS

By FRED SIMON

Medium Folk Rock

Pedal to taste

Repeat and Fade

WEDDING RAIN

By LIZ STORY

4th time to Coda III

2nd time to Coda I;
3rd time to Coda II

D.S. al Coda I

CODA I

espressivo

mp

D.S. al Coda II

CODA II

112

D.S. al Coda III

CODA III